This book belongs to:

____

Made in the USA
Coppell, TX
13 November 2019

11299283R00066